My 60 Seconds

By Deborah Knapp

My 60 Seconds

Illustrated by Robin Davis

ISBN: 0-9741858-7-6

Published by

2525 W Anderson Lane, Suite 540
Austin, Texas 78757

Tel: 512.407.8876
Fax: 512.478.2117

E-mail: info@turnkeypress.com
Web: www.turnkeypress.com

Do's and Don'ts
for Using This Book

Parents:

- Do encourage your children to read a page every day and pray.
- Do encourage your children to finish writing the prayer, IF THEY WANT TO!
- Do set the example by having some time with the Lord each day and then sharing it with your children.
- Don't snoop in their books. It's between them and God.
- Don't expect them to always or even ever share their time with you.
- Do talk with your children about how to respond to others when they ask about the book or ask about what they do during their 60 seconds.
- Do pray really hard for your children. School is tough and this is a new thing for them.

Children:

- Do read a page every day and pray.
- Do finish writing a prayer, ONLY IF YOU WANT TO! Feel free to "pray in your head" as my daughter says. Your God does not need to see it on paper. He has already seen it in your heart!
- Do share with others what you pray if you feel comfortable and think the Lord wants you to.
- Don't do anything with this book that makes you feel uncomfortable or bad.
- Don't worry if you run out of time and you are not finished praying or writing. God understands. You can finish at home or you can finish in your head. Remember, God knows absolutely everything!
- Do pray about everything. God wants to hear it all.

One final note to the children:

One of the things that God really wants is for us to truly enjoy Him. I hope with all my heart you will enjoy your 60 seconds with Him each day. I will be praying for that!

Forward

I have loved Jesus for as long as I remember. My favorite songs still are "Jesus Loves Me" and "This Little Light of Mine, I'm Gonna Let it Shine." When I was eight years old, I made the biggest decision of my life - to follow Jesus, to make him Lord of my life. I remember the day. I remember what I wore when I walked down the aisle. I remember what I prayed with my minister. I was so excited about my decision and being baptized. I wanted to look so beautiful for Jesus. My mother bought me a new dress and took me to the beauty parlor. I was so proud, and I couldn't wait to tell all my friends at school about Jesus and my baptism.

When my youngest daughter made her decision last year, I shared my memories with her. When I finished, she looked up at me sadly and said, "No one at my school will even care. It's against the rules to talk about Jesus."

It has been decades since God was welcomed into our public schools. Now, as of September 1, 2003, our children have 60 seconds each school day to spend with our Lord. Senate Bill 83 was passed by the 78th Regular Session of the Texas Legislature in the spring of 2003. This law provides the 60 seconds to our children.

So how did this book come about? I began talking with my daughter about this new law and how wonderful it was and how it would be a change in her school day. This started out as a journal for her. But as the spring ended and summer arrived, I began realizing that very few people knew about this law including teachers, ministers, and most of my friends. I began wondering, *will our children be prepared? Will they know what to do or how to answer the question, "What do you do during your 60 seconds?"* My true desire is that each child use their 60 seconds each day to simply plug in and let God touch their hearts, open their eyes, and fill their minds with His love and His wisdom. I want our children to know that Jesus loves them, and I want them to let their little lights shine!

Deborah

For Rebekah,
Enjoy your time with Jesus! He loves you so!
From,
Mom

Special thanks to the 78th Texas Legislature.

Day 1

In the beginning God created
the heavens and the earth.

Genesis 1:1 NIV

Dear God,
Thank you for new beginnings! Thank you
for this new school year, my family, my
teachers and my friends! Most of all, thank
you for this time I have with you! Today, Lord,
please bless ...

_____

_____

_____

_____

In Jesus' name I pray. Amen.

I will call to you whenever trouble strikes, and you will help me.

Psalm 86:7 TLB

Dear God,
I am glad I can call on you when I am in trouble, and you will help me. Today, Lord, please help me ...

_____

_____

_____

_____

In Jesus' name I pray. Amen.

Day 2

Day 3

Come to me and live.

Amos 5:4

Dear God,
I do come to you because I want the life you have for me. Today, Lord, I praise you …

_____

_____

_____

_____

In Jesus' name I pray. Amen.

Praise!

Ask, and God will give to you. Search, and you will find. Knock, and the door will open for you.

Matthew 7: 7

Dear God,
I praise you because you delight in giving to me. I ask, I seek, and I am knocking. I am glad the door is always open. Today, Lord, I thank you …

_____

_____

_____

_____

In Jesus' name I pray. Amen.

I will cry to the God
of heaven who does
such wonders for me.

Psalm 57:2 TLB

Dear God,
I can call on you any time. I have a
purpose that is just for me—from you.
Thank you. Today, Lord, please help me ...

_____

_____

_____

_____

In Jesus' name I pray. Amen.

Day 6

See how very much our heavenly Father loves us, for he allows us to be called his children—think of it—and we really are!

1 John 3:1 TLB

Dear God,
I am so thankful that I am yours. No matter how old I get, I will always be your child. Today, Lord, I thank you ...

_____

_____

_____

_____

In Jesus' name I pray. Amen.

If God is with us, no one can defeat us.

Romans 8:31

Dear God,
I am glad you are on my side. I know I am
a winner because I am on your team.
Today, Lord, I thank you …

_____

_____

_____

_____

In Jesus' name I pray. Amen.

Day 8

Don't be afraid, because I have saved you. I have called you by name, and you are mine.

Isaiah 43:1

Dear God,
I am saved, you know me, and I am yours.
Today, Lord, I praise you …

_____

_____

_____

_____

In Jesus' name I pray. Amen.

Day 9

Dear God,
I feel wonderful knowing that you will
love me always and forever. Today, Lord, I
thank you …

_____

_____

_____

_____

In Jesus' name I pray. Amen.

I love you people with a
love that will last forever.
Jeremiah 31:3

Now begin the work, and may
the Lord be with you.

1 Chronicles 22:16

Dear God,
I am ready to work, and I sure am glad you are
with me! Today, Lord, please help me ...

_____

_____

_____

_____

In Jesus' name I pray. Amen.

Day 11

Dear God,
I am thankful that you have always known me and that I am special to you. You have always known who and where I would be. Thank you for placing me here and now. Today, Lord, I praise you …

_____

_____

_____

_____

In Jesus' name I pray. Amen.

Before I formed you in the womb, I knew you.

Jeremiah 1:5

Praise!

God has made us what we are. In Christ Jesus, God made us to do good works, which God planned in advance for us to live our lives doing.

Ephesians 2:10

Dear God,
Thank you for my life. I want to do the good work you have planned for me. I do not always know what it is. Please show me. Today, Lord, please forgive me ...

_____

_____

_____

_____

In Jesus' name I pray. Amen.

Day 13

I pray that your hearts will be
flooded with light so that you
can see something of the future
he has called you to share.

Ephesians 1:18 TLB

Dear God,
I want to know who you want me to be and what
you want me to do. I trust your purpose for me is
good. Sometimes it is hard to stay focused. Today,
Lord, please help me ...

_____

_____

_____

_____

In Jesus' name I pray. Amen.

And since we are his
children, everything he has
belongs to us, for that is
God's plan.

Galatians 4:7 TLB

Dear God,
I sure like your plan. It is amazing! I cannot
begin to understand what it means to be
your child and get everything you have. Today,
Lord, I praise you ...

_____

_____

_____

_____

In Jesus' name I pray. Amen.

But Lord, you are our Father. We are like clay, and you are the potter. Your hands made us all.

Isaiah 64:8

Dear God,
I am happy to be your clay. Mold me and make me into what you created me to be. Today, Lord, please help me …

_____

_____

_____

_____

In Jesus' name I pray. Amen.

Day 16

From the fullness of his grace, we have all received one blessing after another.

John 1:16 NIV

Dear God,
I know I do not always realize it, but I am very lucky. There are blessings all around me. Just having this time with you each day is such a blessing. Thank you, God! Today, Lord, please bless …

_____

_____

_____

In Jesus' name I pray. Amen.

Day 17

Dear God,
You have my name on your hand. That is so cool!
Lord, sometimes I feel lonely, but I know you are
always thinking of me and loving me. I feel safe
knowing I am right there in the palm of your hand!
Today, Lord, please help me …

_____

_____

_____

_____

In Jesus' name I pray. Amen.

I will not forget you.
See, I have written
your name on my
hand.

Isaiah 49:16

O Lord, you have examined my heart and know everything about me. You know when I sit or stand. When far away you know my every thought. You chart the path ahead of me and tell me where to stop and rest. Every moment, you know where I am.

Psalm 139:1-3 TLB

Dear God,
These are wonderful words. Thank you for often reminding me that you are always with me. It is awesome to know that you created me and know everything about me. Today, Lord, I praise you …

_____

_____

_____

_____

In Jesus' name I pray. Amen.

Day 19

Dear God,
You are my mighty God, and I shout for joy! Today, Lord, I praise you …

_____

_____

_____

_____

In Jesus' name I pray. Amen.

The Lord's right hand has done mighty things!

Psalm 118:15 NIV

People ought to enjoy every day of their lives, no matter how long they live.

Ecclesiastes 11:8

Dear God,
I am glad to be alive, and I ask for a happy day. I hope to enjoy all you send my way. Today, Lord, please bless ...

_____

_____

_____

_____

In Jesus' name I pray. Amen.

"I came to give life—life in all its fullness."

John 10:10

Dear God,
I want a full life, and I am thankful you want that for me, too. There are people who think you want to take fun things away. That is a lie. You only want what is best for me. Thank you for loving me in my best interest. Today, Lord, I thank you ...

_____

_____

_____

_____

In Jesus' name I pray. Amen.

Dear God,
It seems like there is a lot of worry
everywhere. Sometimes it is hard not to worry,
but I will try. I trust you with all my heart. Today,
Lord, please help me …

_____

_____

_____

_____

                    In Jesus' name I pray. Amen.

"So don't be anxious about
tomorrow. God will take
care of your tomorrow, too.
Live one day at a time."

                    Matthew 6:34 TLB

Day 23

"I will not leave you as
orphans; I will come to you."
John 14:18 NIV

Dear God,
I believe you and I am not afraid. I am sad for
people who feel alone. Please help them. Today,
Lord, please bless ...

_____

_____

_____

_____

In Jesus' name I pray. Amen.

Be joyful always.

1 Thessalonians 5:16 NIV

Dear God,
I am glad you want this. I will be happy and joyful just as you have asked. Today, Lord, I praise you ...

_____

_____

_____

_____

In Jesus' name I pray. Amen.

Dear God,
Trouble and problems are no fun. Problems are hard to deal with, but I feel better knowing you will help me. I am not afraid because nothing is too hard for you! Today, Lord, please help me ...

_____

_____

_____

_____

In Jesus' name I pray. Amen.

"In this world you will have trouble, but be brave! I have defeated the world."

John 16:33

Day 26

"I am leaving you with a gift—peace of mind and heart! So don't be troubled or afraid".

Dear God,
Peace of mind is a great gift! We all need to take advantage of it. I know I will, and I promise I won't put that gift in my closet on a shelf. Today, Lord, I thank you...

_____

_____

_____

_____

In Jesus' name I pray. Amen.

We know these things are true by
believing, not by seeing.

2 Corinthians 5:7 TLB

Dear God,
I believe YOU! I do not need to see anything,
because I know you always tell the truth. Today,
Lord, I praise you ...

_____

_____

_____

_____

In Jesus' name I pray. Amen.

Day 27

Day 28

A happy heart makes the face
cheerful;

Proverbs 15:13 NIV

Dear God,
I get it. My heart controls my face. You live in my
heart, and I sure hope my face shows it. Today, Lord, I
thank you ...

_____

_____

_____

_____

In Jesus' name I pray. Amen.

Day 29

He has taken our sins away from us as far as the east is from the west.

Psalm 103:12

Dear God,
How do you do that? I wish I could forget mistakes—mine and everyone else's. I am glad you forgive me and that you actually remove all my mistakes. You are truly wonderful! Today, Lord, I thank you …

_____

_____

_____

_____

In Jesus' name I pray. Amen.

Forget all that—it is nothing
compared to what I'm going to do!

Isaiah 43:18 TLB

Dear God,
It is hard to look forward sometimes. My mistakes
make me afraid and my successes make me proud.
But I can't wait to see what all you are going to do.
Today, Lord, please forgive me ...

_____

_____

_____

_____

In Jesus' name I pray. Amen.

Day 30

"Come to me and I will give you rest."

Matthew 11:28 TLB

Dear God,
I do get very tired. I am so thankful I can come to
you any time, and you will give me the rest I need to
make it. Today, Lord, I praise you ...

_____

_____

_____

_____

In Jesus' name I pray. Amen.

Day 32

"Don't be sad, because the joy of
the Lord will make you strong."

Nehemiah 8:10

Dear God,
I will not be sad because you really are my
strength. Instead, I will celebrate. Today,
Lord, I praise you ...

_____

_____

_____

_____

In Jesus' name I pray. Amen.

Day 33

I was in trouble, so I called to the Lord. The Lord answered me and set me free.

Psalm 118:5

Dear God,
Wow, with you as my helper, how can I fail? And when I do, I know you will always be there for me! Today, Lord, I praise you …

_____

_____

_____

_____

In Jesus' name I pray. Amen.

Yes, all have sinned.

Romans 3:23 TLB

Dear God,
It makes me sad to know I mess up and disappoint you. I do trust in Jesus, and I thank you for forgiving me. I am glad that no matter what I do, I can come to you with my broken heart, and you will show me the way back. You will wash me up and send me out clean again. Today, Lord, please forgive me ...

_____

_____

_____

_____

In Jesus' name I pray. Amen.

You will have courage because you will have hope.

Job 11:18 TLB

Dear God,
I count on the hope because I count on you. You never fail me! Today, Lord, I praise you ...

_____

_____

_____

_____

In Jesus' name I pray. Amen.

Day 35

Day 36

"I know what I am planning for you," says the Lord. "I have good plans for you, not plans to hurt you. I will give you hope and a good future."

Jeremiah 29:11

Dear God,
With all my heart, I seek you and the plans you have for me. I know your plan for me is good. I know my future with you is filled with treasures I can only begin to imagine. Today, Lord, please help me ...

_____

_____

_____

_____

In Jesus' name I pray. Amen.

Day 37

But you can trust God, who will not permit you to be tempted more than you can stand. But when you are tempted, he will also give you a way to escape so that you will be able to stand it.

1 Corinthians 10:13

Dear God,
This is good to know because I do not want to mess up. I want to always look to you for help when I am tempted to do wrong. Sometimes things happen so fast, I do not think, and I forget to ask for your help. I am sorry. Today, Lord, please forgive me …

_____

_____

_____

_____

In Jesus' name I pray. Amen.

Dear God,
I do not want to fall. I want to be secure and walk the path you have planned for me. Today, Lord, please help me ...

_____

_____

_____

_____

In Jesus' name I pray. Amen.

A good man has firm footing, but a crook will slip and fall.

Proverbs 10:9 TLB

Before the mountains were born and before you created the earth and the world, you are God. You have always been, and you will always be.

Psalm 90:2

Dear God,
That is a really long time, and I'm going to be right there with you! Today, Lord, I praise you ...

_____

_____

_____

_____

In Jesus' name I pray. Amen.

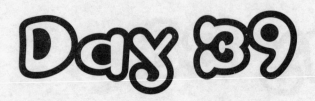

Day 40

We have freedom now because Christ
made us free.

Galatians 5:1

Dear God,
I do thank you for the freedom you have given me. I
want everyone to have this freedom. Today, Lord,
please bless ...

_____

_____

_____

_____

In Jesus' name I pray. Amen.

Day 41

Happy are those who live pure lives,
who follow the Lord's teachings.

Psalm 119:1

Dear God,
I need some help understanding which things in
this world are not good for me. It is hard when
people around me say this and that is good. Please
give me the wisdom I need to know what is good
for me and what I should stay away from. Today,
Lord, please help me ...

_____

_____

_____

_____

In Jesus' name I pray. Amen.

Dear God,
I do believe you will take care of me because you
know my heart. You know I love you. Today, Lord,
please forgive me ...

_____

_____

_____

_____

In Jesus' name I pray. Amen.

You should have confidence
because you respect God;

Job 4:6

Day 42

Day 43

A gentle answer will calm a person's anger, but an unkind answer will cause more anger.

Proverbs 15:1

Dear God,
I hate it when people say mean things to me or holler. I ask that all my words today be kind and gentle. Today, Lord, please help me ...

_____

_____

_____

_____

In Jesus' name I pray. Amen.

You have preserved me because I was honest; you have admitted me forever to your presence.

Psalm 41:12 TLB

Dear God,
I want to be with you. I want to tell the truth always so you will be proud to have me in your presence. Today, Lord, I thank you …

_____

_____

_____

_____

In Jesus' name I pray. Amen.

Dear God,
You save me, love me, and forgive me. What more can
I ask? Today, Lord, I praise you …

_____

_____

_____

_____

In Jesus' name I pray. Amen.

You have forgiven all
my sins.
Isaiah 38:17 TLB

Day 46

Hatred stirs up trouble, but love forgives all wrongs.

Proverbs 10:12

Dear God,
I know it is wrong to hate. To be like you, I know I must love everyone, even when they are not nice to me. That is really hard. Today, Lord, please forgive me ...

_____

_____

_____

_____

In Jesus' name I pray. Amen.

Day 47

Dear God,
I want to be wise not foolish, but I'm going to need some help. Please help me listen to my parents better. Today, Lord, please forgive me ...

_____

_____

_____

In Jesus' name I pray. Amen.

Only a fool despises his father's advice; a wise son considers each suggestion.

Proverbs 15:5 TLB

"Don't criticize, and then you won't be criticized. Others will treat you the way you treat them."

Matthew 7:1-2 TLB

Dear God,
I need to work on this. It is so easy to find things wrong with others. There are times when I think I am better than others. I am so sorry. Today, Lord, please forgive me ...

_____

_____

_____

_____

In Jesus' name I pray. Amen.

For since the world began no one has seen or heard of such a God as ours, who works for those who wait for him!

Isaiah 64:4 TLB

Dear God,
You are so awesome! I will wait for you because I know I can always count on you to give me what I need. You always come through. After all, there is nothing you cannot do. Today, Lord, I praise you …

_____

_____

_____

_____

In Jesus' name I pray. Amen.

Day 50

Dear God,
I want your protection. I want to stand strong for you. My faith in you is strong. Every day I believe you more and more. Today, Lord, please help me ...

_____

_____

_____

_____

In Jesus' name I pray. Amen.

If you want me to protect you, you must learn to believe what I say.

Isaiah 7:9 TLB

Day 51

Christ accepted you, so
you should accept
each other, which will
bring glory to God.

Romans 15:7

Dear God,
I need help accepting everyone around me. It is
not easy to accept people sometimes. But as hard
as it is, I really want to please you. Today, Lord,
please forgive me ...

_____

_____

_____

_____

In Jesus' name I pray. Amen.

There are six things the LORD hates;
There are seven things he cannot stand:
a proud look, a lying tongue, hands that
kill innocent people, a mind that thinks
up evil plans, feet that are quick to do
evil, a witness who lies, and someone
who starts arguments among families.

Proverbs 6:16-19

Dear God,
I do not want my name listed by any of these. I would
be so sad to know I had done something you hated.
Today, Lord, please help me ...

_____

_____

_____

_____

In Jesus' name I pray. Amen.

Day 53

Dear God,
I want to live a life of love like Jesus. I want to love others like you do. Please teach me. Today, Lord, please bless …

_____

_____

_____

_____

In Jesus' name I pray. Amen.

Be full of love for others, following the example of Christ.

Ephesians 5:2 TLB

Sing to the Lord, declare each day that he is the one who saves! Show his glory to the nations! Tell everyone about his miracles!

1 Chronicles 16:23-24 TLB

Dear God,
I praise your wonders. You are the one who saves! You are too wonderful for my words, but I will tell everyone I know anyway! Today, Lord, I praise you ...

_____

_____

_____

_____

In Jesus' name I pray. Amen.

I know, my God, that you test people's hearts. You are happy when people do what is right.

1 Chronicles 29:17

Dear God,
As you test me, I pray you are pleased with what you see. Today, Lord, please help me ...

_____

_____

_____

_____

In Jesus' name I pray. Amen.

Day 56

Dear God,
Teach me to love the way you do. I have so much to learn. Today, Lord, please bless ...

_____

_____

_____

_____

In Jesus' name I pray. Amen.

"Love each other just as much as I love you."

John 13:34 TLB

Day 57

I will sing to you and not be silent. Lord, my God, I will praise you forever.

Psalm 30:12

Dear God,
Thank you for my life and all that I am and have. If I listed all you have given me, it would take forever. Today, Lord, I praise you ...

_____

_____

_____

_____

In Jesus' name I pray. Amen.

People can make all kinds
of plans, but only the Lord's
plan will happen.

Proverbs 19:21

Dear God,
I do have plans, but I want to fulfill your purpose
for me more than I want my plans. I know your
purpose is much more wonderful than any plans I
may have. I will be happy with your decision. Today,
Lord, please help me ...

_____

_____

_____

_____

In Jesus' name I pray. Amen.

Day 59

Dear children, let's stop just saying we love people; let us really love them, and show it by our actions.

1 John 3:18 TLB

Dear God,

I know this is a big deal to you. It is so much easier to say the right words than to do the right actions. I want to do both. Please help me. Today, Lord, please forgive me ...

_____

_____

_____

_____

In Jesus' name I pray. Amen.

Get along with each other, and forgive each other. If someone does wrong to you, forgive that person because the Lord forgave you.

Colossians 3:13

Dear God,
It is tough to forgive like you do. I know I mess up. Oh Lord, please teach me. Today, Lord, please forgive me …

_____

_____

_____

In Jesus' name I pray. Amen.

Dear God,
I know you hate gossip and talking bad about
people. I will do my best to remember that
when I say something ugly, two things happen: I
make you sad, and someone can now say
something ugly about me and it will be the truth.
Today, Lord, please forgive me ...

_____

_____

_____

_____

In Jesus' name I pray. Amen.

Don't use bad language. Say only what is
good and helpful to those you are talking
to.

Ephesians 4:29 TLB

Day 62

Dear God,
Your love is so amazing; It is so complete. I can only begin to imagine. I want more! Today, Lord, I praise you …

_____

_____

_____

_____

In Jesus' name I pray. Amen.

For great is your love, higher than the heavens; your faithfulness reaches to the skies.

Psalm 108:4 NIV

Day 63

Five sparrows are sold for only two pennies, and God does not forget any of them. But God even knows how many hairs you have on your head. Don't be afraid, you are worth much more than many sparrows.

Luke 12:6-7

Dear God,
I am glad I am worth more to you than birds. You do not forget all the birds, and you even know how much hair I have. You are incredible! Thank you for remembering me, and thank you for seeing me as valuable to you. Today, Lord, please bless …

_____

_____

_____

_____

In Jesus' name I pray. Amen.

Always be willing to listen and slow to speak. Do not become angry easily because anger will not help you live the right kind of life God wants.

James 1:19-20

Dear God,
It is so easy to get mad and yell. I want to be better at listening and keeping my cool. Today, Lord, please help me ...

_____

_____

_____

_____

In Jesus' name I pray. Amen.

Day 64

Day 65

Do not let evil defeat you, but defeat evil by doing good.

Romans 12:21

Dear God,
That is a great plan. You are my model. I want to stay close to you and learn. Show me. Teach me. Today, Lord, please help me ...

_____

_____

_____

_____

In Jesus' name I pray. Amen.

A wise man is mightier than a strong man. Wisdom is mightier than strength.

Proverbs 24:5 TLB

Dear God,
No matter how old I get and no matter how much I understand, there will always be more to learn. I want wisdom and understanding. Today, Lord, please help me ...

_____

_____

_____

_____

In Jesus' name I pray. Amen.

Whoever does not love
does not know God,
because God is love.

1 John 4:8

Dear God,
You are love, and I want to know you more and
more every day. When people see me, I want
them to know that I know you. Today, Lord, I
praise you ...

_____

_____

_____

_____

In Jesus' name I pray. Amen.

Day 68

Sing to him; sing praises to him.
Tell all about his miracles.

1 Chronicles 16:9

Dear God,
I do thank you for everything. I praise you, and I
want to tell everyone I know all about you. Today,
Lord, please bless ...

_____

_____

_____

_____

In Jesus' name I pray. Amen.

Day 69

Dear God,
All of your creation is good, and I am thankful. Everywhere I look I see you busy at work. I pray for my family, my friends, my teachers, my country and the whole world. I ask you to give us what we need. Today, Lord, I praise you ...

_____

_____

_____

_____

In Jesus' name I pray. Amen.

First, I tell you to pray for all people, asking God for what they need and being thankful to him.

1 Timothy 2:1

For God has said, "I will never, never fail you nor forsake you." That is why we can say without any doubt or fear, "The Lord is my helper, and I am not afraid of anything that mere man can do to me."

Hebrews 13:5-6 TLB

Dear God,
I am so glad I will never be alone because you promise to never leave me. You are my greatest helper, and I will not be afraid. Today, Lord, I praise you ...

_____

_____

_____

_____

In Jesus' name I pray. Amen.

Day 71

Dear God,
I don't want to be a fake. Sometimes evil is disguised as
good. Teach me to recognize the difference. I want to be
on the right side. Today, Lord, please help me ...

_____

_____

_____

_____

In Jesus' name I pray. Amen.

Your love must be real.
Hate what is evil. Hold
on to what is good.
Romans 12:9

I will sing to the Lord
because he has taken
care of me.

Psalm 13:6

Dear God,
You really have been so good to me, and I thank you
with all my heart. Today, Lord, I praise you ...

_____

_____

_____

_____

In Jesus' name I pray. Amen.

Day 73

Dear God,
I want to help others like you help me. Please show me how and give me opportunities. Today, Lord, please bless ...

_____

_____

_____

_____

                    In Jesus' name I pray. Amen.

Share each other's troubles
and problems, and obey
our Lord's commands.

Galatians 6:2 TLB

Listen to advice and accept
instruction, and in the end you
will be wise.

Proverbs 19:20 NIV

Dear God,
I know I have a lot to learn, but I don't always feel like
being taught or corrected. I will work at this. I do
want to be wise. Today, Lord, please forgive me ...

_____

_____

_____

_____

In Jesus' name I pray. Amen.

Day 74

Day 75

We love because God first
loved us.

1 John 4:19

Dear God,
Thank you for loving me first. Thank you for teaching me
how to love. Please keep teaching me. I trust your perfect
love. Today, Lord, I thank you …

_____

_____

_____

_____

In Jesus' name I pray. Amen.

Do not lie to each other.

Colossians 3:9

Dear God,

I know you hate lies and gossip. I will make good choices. Today, Lord, please help me …

_____

_____

_____

_____

In Jesus' name I pray. Amen.

And love means living the way God commanded us to live. As you have heard from the very beginning, his command is this: Live a life of love.

2 John 1:6

Dear God,
Some people think it is not cool to obey, but Lord, I know it is the coolest thing I can do. I will follow you and I will love others. Today, Lord, I praise you …

_____

_____

_____

_____

In Jesus' name I pray. Amen.

Day 78

No one has ever seen God, but if we love each other, God lives in us, and his love is made perfect in us.

1 John 4:12

Dear God,
Your love is forever. It will never go away from me. I promise to do my best loving others because I want to be part of your perfect love. Today, Lord, I praise you …

_____

_____

_____

In Jesus' name I pray. Amen.

Day 79

Dear God,
I know it is wrong to have bad thoughts and think of bad or mean things to do. I never want to be known as a troublemaker. Today, Lord, please forgive me …

_____

_____

_____

_____

In Jesus' name I pray. Amen.

Whoever makes evil plans will be known as a troublemaker.

Proverbs 24:8

So also, the tongue is a small thing but what enormous damage it can do.

James 3:5 TLB

Dear God,
Please teach me to keep my mouth shut when my words will hurt someone. And while you are doing that, could you please help me to not think of bad things to say? Today, Lord, please forgive me ...

_____

_____

_____

_____

In Jesus' name I pray. Amen.

Day 80

Forgive!

My child, listen and accept what I say. Then you will have a long life. I am guiding you in the way of wisdom, and I am leading you on the right path.

Proverbs 4:10-11

Dear God,
I want a long and good life. Please help me listen and do what you say. Lord, I trust you to lead me where I should go. Today, Lord, I thank you …

_____

_____

_____

_____

In Jesus' name I pray. Amen.

Sing praise to the Lord because he has done great things. Let all the world know what he has done.

Isaiah 12:5

Dear God,
The wonderful things you have done are too many to name. If I could, I would sing your praises out loud right now. Today, Lord, I praise you …

_____

_____

_____

_____

In Jesus' name I pray. Amen.

Day 82

The Word became a human and lived among us. We saw his glory—the glory that belongs to the only Son of the Father—and he was full of grace and truth.

John 1:14

.

Dear God,
All I can say is thank you! I praise you, and I am so glad you are my God! Today, Lord, I praise you ...

_____

_____

_____

_____

In Jesus' name I pray. Amen.

Day 84

Be glad for all God is
planning for you.

Romans 12:12 TLB

Dear God,
I am not just glad, I am excited about the plans you
have for me. Just show me the way. I cannot wait to
see what all you have in store for me. Today, Lord, I
praise you ...

_____

_____

_____

_____

In Jesus' name I pray. Amen.

Day 85

Dear God,
I get it. I am following you! You lead the way and I will tag along. Today, Lord, please help me …

_____

_____

_____

_____

In Jesus' name I pray. Amen.

Let us decide for ourselves
what is right, and let us learn
together what is good.

Job 34:4

Any story sounds true until someone tells the other side and sets the record straight.

Proverbs 18:17 TLB

Dear God,
This is tricky because I hear so many things from other people. I do not always hear both sides. I do not always ask and I am sorry. I do know that you always tell the truth. Help me make good choices. Today, Lord, I thank you …

_____

_____

_____

_____

In Jesus' name I pray. Amen.

Day 87

Don't talk so much. You keep putting your foot in your mouth. Be sensible and turn off the flow.

Proverbs 10:19 TLB

Dear God,
Please make my words few. I want to keep my feet on the ground and out of my mouth. Today, Lord, please help me …

_____

_____

_____

_____

In Jesus' name I pray. Amen.

Love is patient and kind.
Love is not jealous, it does
not brag and it is not
proud.

1 Corinthians 13:4

Dear God,
That is a tall order. The way you love is patient, kind, and humble. Please teach me. I really want to love the way you do. Today, Lord, please help me …

_____

_____

_____

_____

In Jesus' name I pray. Amen.

Day 88

Let us please the other fellow, not ourselves, and do what is for his good and build him up in the Lord.

Romans 15:2 TLB

Dear God,
There are people all around me who need my help. I want to help others your way. Today, Lord, please bless …

_____

_____

_____

_____

In Jesus' name I pray. Amen.

Day 90

Do everything in love.

1 Corinthians 16:14

Dear God,
That sounds simple, but it is not always easy. Please
teach me. Today, Lord, please help me ...

_____

_____

_____

_____

In Jesus' name I pray. Amen.

Day 91

Don't become angry quickly, because getting angry is foolish.

Ecclesiastes 7:9

Dear God,
You are right! It is foolish to get angry quickly and let someone else control how I act. Today, Lord, please forgive me ...

_____

_____

_____

_____

In Jesus' name I pray. Amen.

The intelligent person is always open to new ideas and learning. In fact, he looks for them.

Proverbs 18:15 TLB

Dear God,
I have a lot to learn, and sometimes I don't like change. I am going to work hard to learn all I can and be open to all the new ideas you send my way. Today, Lord, please help me ...

_____

_____

_____

_____

In Jesus' name I pray. Amen.

Day 92

Day 93

Children, obey your parents in all things, because this pleases the Lord.

Colossians 3:20

Dear God,
I really mess up here sometimes. I know they love me very much, and I do not want to disappoint them or you. Today, Lord, please forgive me ...

_____

_____

_____

_____

In Jesus' name I pray. Amen.

Anyone who loves learning accepts correction, but a person who hates being corrected is stupid.

Proverbs 12:1

Dear God,
This one is hard to take sometimes. I know I have a lot to learn. Please teach me the wisdom of learning and that correction helps me. Today, Lord, please forgive me ...

_____

_____

_____

_____

In Jesus' name I pray. Amen.

Then listen to me; be quiet, and I
will teach you wisdom.

Job 33:33

Dear God,
I am quiet, and I am listening. Please teach me
wisdom. Today, Lord, I thank you ...

_____

_____

_____

_____

In Jesus' name I pray. Amen.

Day 96

A good man's mind is filled with honest thoughts; an evil man's mind is crammed with lies.

Proverbs 12:5 TLB

Dear God,
Teach me to know and recognize the difference between the truth and a lie. I want my mind to be filled with only truth. Today, Lord, please help me ...

_____

_____

_____

_____

 In Jesus' name I pray. Amen.

Day 97

"Then you will know the truth, and the truth will set you free."

John 8:32 NIV

Dear God,
You are the truth. I want to know
you better and be free. Today,
Lord, I praise you ...

_____

_____

_____

_____

In Jesus' name I pray. Amen.

So encourage each other and give each other strength.

1 Thessalonians 5:11

Dear God,
I want to learn how to encourage and build others up—just like you do. I need you to keep showing me how. Today, Lord, please bless …

_____

_____

_____

In Jesus' name I pray. Amen.

Day 99

It is possible to give away and become richer! It is also possible to hold on too tightly and lose everything.

Proverbs 11:24 TLB

Dear God,
You know I would not mind being rich, but I want to be generous with others because it is your way. Today, Lord, please bless …

_____

_____

_____

_____

In Jesus' name I pray. Amen.

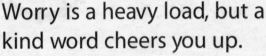

Worry is a heavy load, but a
kind word cheers you up.

Proverbs 12:25

Dear God,
Nice words do make me feel better. I will look for
people to encourage today so their hearts will not be
heavy. I will start with my family, my friends and my
teachers. Today, Lord, please bless ...

_____

_____

_____

_____

In Jesus' name I pray. Amen.

The Lord hates those who
tell lies but is pleased with
those who keep their
promises.

Proverbs 12:22

Dear God,
I will try hard to keep the promises I make. I
pray you are delighted with me. Today, Lord,
please forgive me ...

_____

_____

_____

_____

In Jesus' name I pray. Amen.

Day 102

You have no right to criticize your
brother or look down on him.

Romans 14:10 TLB

Dear God,
I will try very hard today to make decisions and
choices that will keep the peace wherever I am. I
will look for good in people, not bad. Today, Lord,
please help me ...

_____

_____

_____

_____

In Jesus' name I pray. Amen.

Day 103

Dear God,
Choosing friends is a huge decision. Friends are so important, but good friends are even more important. You are my best friend because you love me no matter what, and you are always there for me. Today, Lord, I thank you ...

_____

_____

_____

_____

In Jesus' name I pray. Amen.

There are "friends" who pretend to be friends, but there is a friend who sticks closer than butter.

Proverbs 18:24 TLB

Do not let anyone treat you as if you were unimportant.

Titus 2:15

Dear God,
I am so glad I am important to you. Thank you for the Bible. I know it is the truth. Reading your words and praying to you help me, and I am thankful I can do this every day! Today, Lord, I praise you …

_____

_____

_____

_____

In Jesus' name I pray. Amen.

Day 105

When I am afraid, I
will trust you.

Psalm 56:3

Dear God,
I will always trust in you when I am afraid.
In fact, I am just going to trust you all the
time, because you are faithful! Today, Lord, I
thank you ...

_____

_____

_____

_____

In Jesus' name I pray. Amen.

When the Holy Spirit controls our lives, he will produce this kind of fruit in us: love, joy, peace, patience, kindness, goodness, faithfulness, gentleness and self-control.

Galatians 5:22-23 TLB

Dear God,
I want a huge bowl of the Spirit's fruit of love, joy, peace, patience, kindness, goodness, faithfulness, gentleness and self-control. Please, Lord, fill me up. Giving up control is sometimes tough, but I want the Holy Spirit to take and keep control. Today, Lord, please help me ...

_____

_____

_____

_____

In Jesus' name I pray. Amen.

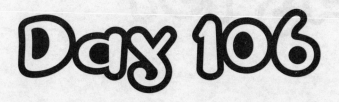

Day 106

A dull axe means harder work.
Being wise will make it easier.

Ecclesiastes 10:10

Dear God,
I get it. The more I learn, the wiser I get. The wiser I get, the easier life is. Today, Lord, I thank you …

_____

_____

_____

_____

In Jesus' name I pray. Amen.

Day 108

March on, my soul, with strength!
Judges 5:21

Dear God,
I am so thankful that as I march on you will
be with me to give me strength. Stay close to
me. Today, Lord, I praise you …

_____

_____

_____

_____

In Jesus' name I pray. Amen.

Day 109

Dear God,
I will do my best to do for others as you do for me. I want everyone to see you working in me. Today, Lord, please bless ...

_____

_____

_____

_____

In Jesus' name I pray. Amen.

I have freely and happily become a servant to any and all so that I can win them to Christ.

1 Corinthians 9:19 TLB

God's word is alive and working and is sharper than a double-edged sword.

Hebrews 4:12

Dear God,
Wow! I know there is great power in your word. I know I cannot understand that power, but I will listen. I want to be on the side of good—the one that wins. Today, Lord, I praise you ...

_____

_____

_____

_____

In Jesus' name I pray. Amen.

Day 111

There are three things that continue forever: faith, hope and love. And the greatest of these is love.

1 Corinthians 13:13

Dear God,
You have taught me that above everything else, love is the greatest gift I can give. I want to love your way Lord. Today, Lord, please help me ...

_____

_____

_____

_____

In Jesus' name I pray. Amen.

Everyone enjoys giving good advice, and how wonderful it is to be able to say the right thing at the right time!

Proverbs 15:23 TLB

Dear God,
That sure is the truth. Everyone, even I, loves to tell others what to do. Please help me to speak only when it is the right thing at the right time. Today, Lord, please forgive me ...

_____

_____

_____

_____

In Jesus' name I pray. Amen.

Let love and faithfulness never leave you; bind them around your neck, write them on the tablet of your heart.

Proverbs 3:3 NIV

Dear God,
With all the love and faithfulness you show me, I will never forget their importance. They will be in my heart always. I will never let them go. Today, Lord, please bless …

_____

_____

_____

_____

In Jesus' name I pray. Amen.

Day 114

For I am convinced that
nothing can separate
us from his love.

Romans 8:38 TLB

Dear God,
You are the one for me. No matter what, you are
always there for me, loving me. If I don't feel it, I
know it's because I'm not looking your way. Today,
Lord, I thank you …

_____

_____

_____

_____

In Jesus' name I pray. Amen.

Day 115

Do not be lazy but work hard, serving the Lord with all your heart.

Romans 12:11

Dear God,
I pray I serve you today in a way that will bring you great delight. Today, Lord, please help me ...

_____

_____

_____

_____

In Jesus' name I pray. Amen.

Dear God,
Sometimes it is hard to stop thinking about me and what
I want. I'm going to try really hard to think about other
people. Today, Lord, please forgive me ...

_____

_____

_____

_____

In Jesus' name I pray. Amen.

Do not be interested only in your own
life, but be interested in the lives of
others.

Philippians 2:4

Day 117

Listen, my son, and be
wise, and keep your heart
on the right path.

Proverbs 23:19

Dear God,
Just show me the way because that is where I want
to go! Today, Lord, please help me ...

_____

_____

_____

_____

In Jesus' name I pray. Amen.

Remaining calm solves
great problems.
Ecclesiastes 10:4

Dear God,
Being calm in this world is sometimes difficult, but I
do want to be part of the solution—not the
problem. Today, Lord, please help me ...

_____

_____

_____

_____

In Jesus' name I pray. Amen.

Share with God's people who need help.

Romans 12:13

Dear God,

I've been told to share my whole life. And now that I think about it, I sure do like it when others share with me. Today, Lord, I thank you ...

_____

_____

_____

_____

In Jesus' name I pray. Amen.

Day 119

Day 120

If someone mistreats you because you are a Christian, don't curse him, pray that God will bless him.

Romans 12:14 TLB

Dear God,
It is really hard to ask that a good thing be given to someone who has been mean to me, but I trust you and I will try. Today, Lord, please help me ...

_____

_____

_____

_____

In Jesus' name I pray. Amen.

Day 121

Dear God,
There are so many bad choices I can make
and problems are hard. I want to trust and
not be afraid. I know you are always with me.
Today, Lord, please help me …

_____

_____

_____

_____

In Jesus' name I pray. Amen.

Happy is the man who doesn't give in
and do wrong when he is tempted.

James 1:12 TLB

I can do all things through Christ,
because he gives me strength.

Philippians 4:13

Dear God,
You are my strength. I know with you I can
do anything that is in your will. Today, Lord, I
praise you ...

_____

_____

_____

_____

In Jesus' name I pray. Amen.

Day 123

Don't brag about tomorrow; you don't know what may happen.

Proverbs 27:1

Dear God,
I remember you hate bragging. I will keep in mind that all I have comes straight from you, and you are in control. Today, Lord, please forgive me ...

_____

_____

_____

In Jesus' name I pray. Amen.

His purpose in all of this is that they should seek after God and perhaps feel their way toward him and find him— though he is not far from any one of us.

Acts 17:27 TLB

Dear God,
It is wonderful to know you are not far from me. I do seek you and want to find you every day. Today, Lord, I thank you ...

_____

_____

_____

_____

In Jesus' name I pray. Amen.

Dear God,
I trust you, and I am not worried or afraid. You show
me blessings all the time. Today, Lord, I praise you …

_____

_____

_____

_____

In Jesus' name I pray. Amen.

But the person who
trusts in the Lord will
be blessed. The Lord
will show him that he
can be trusted.

Jeremiah 17:7

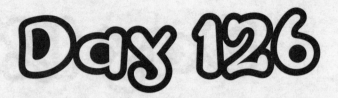

Day 126

Dear God,
I will do my best to be organized and add to peace.
Today, Lord, please help me ...

_____

_____

_____

In Jesus' name I pray. Amen.

God is not a God of confusion but a God of peace.

1 Corinthians 14:33

Day 127

Now stand still and see the great thing
the Lord will do before your eyes.

1 Samuel 12:16

Dear God,
I will be still and watch for you. You do great things
before my eyes every day. Your sunsets are amazing
paintings and are only one example of your many
great miracles. Today, Lord, I thank you ...

_____

_____

_____

_____

In Jesus' name I pray. Amen.

As the deer pants for
the water, so I long for
you, O God.

Psalm 42:1 TLB

Dear God,
I do want to be with you - safe and secure. You are
the one who can help me and show me the way.
Today, Lord, I praise you …

_____

_____

_____

_____

In Jesus' name I pray. Amen.

Day 129

"Your heart will be where your treasure is."

Luke 12:34

Dear God,
My heart is with you and my thoughts are of you because you are my treasure. Today, Lord, I praise you ...

_____

_____

_____

_____

In Jesus' name I pray. Amen.

Work hard and cheerfully at all you do, just as though you are working for the Lord.

Colossians 3:23 TLB

Dear God,
I know you hate laziness. I will work on this, and yes, with all my heart. Today, Lord, please help me ...

_____

_____

_____

_____

In Jesus' name I pray. Amen.

Day 130

God's voice thunders in wonderful ways;
he does great things we cannot
understand.

Job 37:5

Dear God,
I want to understand, but I don't need to
understand. I just need to believe you and I do!
Today, Lord, I praise you …

_____

_____

_____

_____

In Jesus' name I pray. Amen.

Day 131

Day 132

And we know that in everything God works for the good of those who love him.

Romans 8:28

Dear God,
I do love you, and I want to fulfill your purpose for me. I want to fit into your plans. Today, Lord, please help me ...

_____

_____

_____

_____

In Jesus' name I pray. Amen.

Day 133

This is the day the Lord has made; let us rejoice and be glad in it.

Psalm 118:24 NIV

Dear God,
Yes it is and I do rejoice and I am very glad!
Today, Lord, I praise you ...

_____

_____

_____

_____

In Jesus' name I pray. Amen.

So don't worry, because I am with you.
Don't be afraid, because I am your God. I
will make you strong and I will help you;
I will support you with my right hand
that saves you.

Isaiah 41:10

Dear God,
I am counting on you and I know I will be
amazed! Today, Lord, I thank you …

_____

_____

_____

_____

In Jesus' name I pray. Amen.

Fight the good fight of faith, grabbing hold of the life that continues forever.

1 Timothy 6:12

Dear God,
I will and I will win because you are on my side! Today, Lord, please help me ...

_____

_____

_____

_____

In Jesus' name I pray. Amen.

The Lord is good to those who hope in him, to those who seek him. It is good to wait quietly for the Lord to save.

Lamentations 3:25-26

Dear God,
My hope is in you. I wait because you always come. I seek you every day, and every day, you are here with me! Thank you. Today, Lord, I praise you ...

_____

_____

_____

_____

In Jesus' name I pray. Amen.

For God is at work within you, helping you want to obey him and then helping you do what he wants.

Philippians 2:13 TLB

Dear God,
Keep working in me. I do not want to go it alone. Your plan for me is so much better than anything I could come up with. Today, Lord, please help me …

_____

_____

_____

_____

In Jesus' name I pray. Amen.

Day 137

Day 138

So you see, it isn't enough just to have faith. You must also do good to prove that you have it.

James 2:17 TLB

Dear God,
Did you come up with "actions speak louder than words"? I pray that my actions will prove my faith in you. I want everyone to know you are the Lord of my life without me ever having to say a word. Today, Lord, please forgive me ...

_____

_____

_____

_____

In Jesus' name I pray. Amen.

Do not let the sun go
down while you are
still angry.

Ephesians 4:26 NIV

Dear God,
This is a good habit to start and keep. Today, Lord,
please forgive me ...

_____

_____

_____

_____

In Jesus' name I pray. Amen.

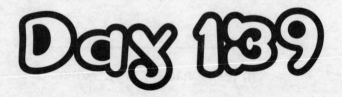

Day 140

So we should control ourselves. We should wear faith and love to protect us, and the hope of salvation should be our helmet.

1 Thessalonians 5:8

Dear God,
These are what I will put on first before I start every day. Today, Lord, please help me ...

_____

_____

_____

_____

In Jesus' name I pray. Amen.

I chose you so you would
know and believe me, so
you would understand
that I am the true God.
There was no God before
me, and there will be no
God after me.

Isaiah 43:10

Dear God,
You are the one and the only! I know it, and I
want to know you better and better. I do
believe you. Today, Lord, I praise you …

_____

_____

_____

_____

In Jesus' name I pray. Amen.

Day 142

What is faith? It is the confident assurance that something we want is going to happen. It is the certainty that what we hope for is waiting for us, even though we cannot see it up ahead.

Hebrews 11:1 TLB

Dear God,
I'm in pretty good shape because I am sure of the hope I have in you, and I am also very certain that you are my awesome God! My hope is totally in you. Today, Lord, I praise you ...

_____

_____

_____

_____

In Jesus' name I pray. Amen.

"I pray for these followers, but I am also praying for all those who will believe in me because of their teaching."

John 17:20

Dear God,
It makes me tremble to know that you prayed for me in the Garden of Gethsemane so long ago. You really do love me and want me for yours! I really want to love you back the same way. Today, Lord, please forgive me ...

_____

_____

_____

_____

In Jesus' name I pray. Amen.

Day 143

Day 144

No longer will you need the sun or moon to give you light, for the Lord your God will be your everlasting light, and he will be your glory.

Isaiah 60:19 TLB

Dear God,
Your promises are so cool. You are my everlasting light, and I feel safe standing in it. I hope you smile when you see me in it. Today, Lord, I praise you …

_____

_____

_____

_____

In Jesus' name I pray. Amen.

Don't envy sinners, but always respect the Lord. Then you will have hope for a future, and your wishes will come true.

Proverbs 23:17-18

Dear God,
I look forward to my future with you as my guide. I do have hope, and my hope is in you! Today, Lord, I thank you …

_____

_____

_____

_____

In Jesus' name I pray. Amen.

Day 146

So our hope is in the Lord, He is our help, our shield to protect us.

Psalm 33:20

Dear God,
I do depend on you because you always come through for me! Today, Lord, I praise you …

_____

_____

_____

_____

In Jesus' name I pray. Amen.

Day 147

The man of few words and settled mind is wise; therefore, even a fool is thought to be wise when he is silent. It pays him to keep his mouth shut.

Proverbs 17:27-28 TLB

Dear God,
I would rather be a wise fool than a smart jerk. You talk a lot about listening. I am working on it. My ears aren't always used as much as my mouth. Today, Lord, please forgive me ...

_____

_____

_____

_____

In Jesus' name I pray. Amen.

Dear God,
My eyes are fixed on you! Today, Lord, I
praise you …

_____

_____

_____

_____

In Jesus' name I pray. Amen.

So we do not look at
what we can see right
now, the troubles all
around us, but we look
forward to the joys in
heaven which we have
not yet seen.

2 Corinthians 4:18

"If you know these things, you will be happy if you do them."

John 13:17

Dear God,
My goal is to do the things you ask. I want happiness and the blessings you promise. Today, Lord, please help me ...

_____

_____

_____

In Jesus' name I pray. Amen.

Day 149

Day 150

But, strange as it seems, we Christians actually do have within us a portion of the very thoughts and mind of Christ.

1 Corinthians 2:16 TLB

Dear God,
You are in me! That is too wonderful. I feel safe knowing you live right here in my heart. I will take great care with my thoughts. Today, Lord, please help me ...

_____

_____

_____

_____

In Jesus' name I pray. Amen.

Day 151

We have troubles all around us, but we are not defeated. We do not know what to do, but we do not give up the hope of living.

2 Corinthians 4:8

Dear God,
Because of you I can get back up again.
Because of you I have hope and I am not afraid! Today, Lord, I praise you ...

_____

_____

_____

_____

In Jesus' name I pray. Amen.

I know that I have not reached that goal, but there is one thing I always do. Forgetting the past and straining toward what is ahead, I keep trying to reach the goal and get the prize for which God called me through Christ to the life above.

Philippians 3:13-14

Dear God,
I will not quit. I will press on to be what you created me to be and reach all the treasures you have for me. Today, Lord, please help me …

_____

_____

_____

_____

In Jesus' name I pray. Amen.

Obey God because you are his children;

1 Peter 1:14 TLB

Dear God,
I pray for your help on this one so much. It is hard. All around me are ideas and thoughts that are not your way. Some people laugh and make fun of the word obey. Today, Lord, please help me ...

_____

_____

_____

_____

In Jesus' name I pray. Amen.

Day 154

And God can give you more blessings
than you need.

2 Corinthians 9:8

Dear God,
It is so wonderful to know that no matter
what is going on, you will provide me with
whatever it is that I need to do my work—
even more. Today, Lord, I thank you ...

_____

_____

_____

_____

In Jesus' name I pray. Amen.

Day 155

The same thing is true of the words I speak. They will not return to me empty. They make the things happen that I want to happen, and they succeed in doing what I send them to do.

Isaiah 55:11

Dear God,
You never lose. I love the words you say! Knowing I am special to you makes me feel so good. I praise you and clap my hands for you. Today, Lord, I praise you ...

_____

_____

_____

_____

In Jesus' name I pray. Amen.

Obey my commands and you will live! Guard my teachings as you would your own eyes.

Proverbs 7:2

Dear God,
It is an honor to guard your teachings in my heart and to know that living by them gives me a full and happy life. Today, Lord, I praise you ...

_____

_____

_____

_____

In Jesus' name I pray. Amen.

Day 156

You only need to remain calm, the Lord will fight for you.

Exodus 14:14

Dear God,
You got it! I will be calm. I will be in your will and I will wait on you. I am glad you are my God and on my side! Today, Lord, I thank you …

_____

_____

_____

_____

In Jesus' name I pray. Amen.

Day 157

Day 158

Don't be afraid! Don't worry! I have always told you what will happen. You are my witnesses. There is no other God but me. I know of no other rock; I am the only one.

Isaiah 44:8

Dear God,
You are my God! Is there anything you cannot do? You are more than I can imagine. I will trust you always. Today, Lord, I thank you …

_____

_____

_____

_____

In Jesus' name I pray. Amen.

What a shame—yes, how stupid!—to decide before knowing the facts!

Proverbs 18:13 TLB

Dear God,
You really understand us, don't you? Your word speaks a great deal about truth and knowing you. Keep talking and I'll keep listening. Today, Lord, please forgive me …

_____

_____

_____

_____

In Jesus' name I pray. Amen.

Day 160

Dear God,
I hear you. You have the plan. I tag along with you, and it all goes perfectly. That is exactly what I want to do! Today, Lord, please help me ...

_____

_____

_____

_____

In Jesus' name I pray. Amen.

Keep your eyes on Jesus, our leader and instructor.

Hebrews 12:2 TLB

Day 161

The everlasting God is
your place of safety,
and his arms will hold
you up forever.

Deuteronomy 33:27

Dear God,
Wow! Knowing I am protected in your arms forever
is more than I can understand, but I know I like it.
Today, Lord, I praise you ...

_____

_____

_____

_____

In Jesus' name I pray. Amen.

A foolish person enjoys doing wrong,
but a person with understanding
enjoys doing what is wise.

Proverbs 10:23

Dear God,
Please take away any foolishness, and fill me
up with understanding and wisdom. Today,
Lord, I thank you …

_____

_____

_____

_____

In Jesus' name I pray. Amen.

But you should be strong. Don't give up, because you will get a reward for your good work.

2 Chronicles 15:7

Dear God,
I will not give up because I know you will reward me for the good work I do. You will reward me with a blessing just for me as long as I am working for you. Today, Lord, I thank you …

_____

_____

_____

_____

In Jesus' name I pray. Amen.

Day 163

Day 164

Dear God,
I want you to be pleased with me more than anything. I want to do good and share out of love, not just because I am supposed to. Today, Lord, please bless ...

_____

_____

_____

_____

In Jesus' name I pray. Amen.

Do not forget to do good for others and share with them because such sacrifices please God.

Hebrews 13:16

Day 165

The Lord himself will go before you. He
will be with you, he will not forget you.

Deuteronomy 31:8

Dear God,
OK, I am ready! I believe you. Let's go! Today,
Lord, I praise you …

_____

_____

_____

In Jesus' name I pray. Amen.

Day 166

But if I were you, I would call on God and bring my problem before him. God does wonders that cannot be understood; he does so many miracles they cannot be counted.

Job 5:8-9

Dear God,
That is great advice! You are my God, and I come to you to confess and for help because I know you can and I know you will be there for me! Today, Lord, I thank you …

_____

_____

_____

_____

In Jesus' name I pray. Amen.

Let everyone see that you are gentle and kind.

Philippians 4:5

Dear God,
I am working on this. I know my actions should never be selfish or rude. I will look for opportunities to practice this. Today, Lord, please forgive me ...

_____

_____

_____

_____

In Jesus' name I pray. Amen.

Day 168

Christ will shine on you.
Ephesians 5:14

Dear God,
You are the light of my life. Shine on me!
Today, Lord, I praise you ...

_____

_____

_____

_____

In Jesus' name I pray. Amen.

Day 169

You know that in a race all the runners run, but only one gets the prize. So run to win!

1 Corinthians 9:24

Dear God,
With you as my coach and the judge of this race, how can I lose? I will run, and I will run with you! Today, Lord, please help me ...

_____

_____

_____

_____

In Jesus' name I pray. Amen.

The Lord will keep you from all harm—he will watch over your life; the Lord will watch over your coming and going both now and forevermore.

Psalm 121:7-8 NIV

Dear God,
I truly am safe with you watching over me and guarding me forever. Thank you! Today, Lord, I praise you …

_____

_____

_____

_____

In Jesus' name I pray. Amen.

Day 170

Always be humble, gentle and patient, accepting each other in love.

Ephesians 4:2

Dear God,
It's so easy for you to be humble and gentle and patient and loving. I will follow your lead. Today, Lord, please forgive me …

_____

_____

_____

_____

In Jesus' name I pray. Amen.

Day 172

The Lord God is my strength. He makes me like a deer that does not stumble so I can walk on the steep mountains.

Habakkuk 3:19

Dear God,
You are the source of any power I have. You are who pushes and pulls me towards success and happiness. I thank you. Today, Lord, I praise you ...

_____

_____

_____

_____

In Jesus' name I pray. Amen.

Day 173

Please, Lord, save us; please,
Lord, give us success.

Psalm 118:25

Dear God,
When I am down, you are there. You help
me. You save me. You really do love me.
Today, Lord, I thank you …

_____

_____

_____

_____

In Jesus' name I pray. Amen.

Dear God,
I feel safe knowing your love is now and
forever. Today, Lord, I praise you ...

_____

_____

_____

In Jesus' name I pray. Amen.

Lord, you do everything for me. Lord,
your love continues forever.

Psalm 138:8

Day 174

May the Lord watch over
you and give you peace.

Numbers 6:26

Dear God,
Your words are so peaceful. I feel the peace
that comes only from you, and I praise you
for your love for me and for everyone. I
want everyone to feel the peace I have in
loving you. Today, Lord, please bless ...

_____

_____

_____

_____

In Jesus' name I pray. Amen.

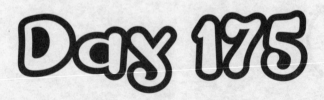

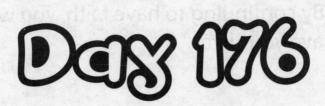

Day 176

So do not be ashamed to
tell people about our
Lord Jesus.

2 Timothy 1:7

Dear God,
Sometimes I am not sure what I am supposed to
say. It is not always comfortable, but I do love you
and I want others to love you also. Today, Lord,
please help me ...

_____

_____

_____

_____

In Jesus' name I pray. Amen.

"By continuing to have faith, you will save your lives."

Luke 21:19

Dear God,
I do have faith. My faith is in you and you alone. I will stand firmly with you! Today, Lord, please help me ...

_____

_____

_____

_____

In Jesus' name I pray. Amen.

Day 177

Day 178

The whole Bible was given to us by inspiration from God and is useful to teach us what is true and to make us realize what is wrong in our lives; it straightens us out and helps us do what is right.

2 Timothy 3:16 TLB

Dear God,
I want to finish what you began in me—a good work. I will always believe you. You always speak the truth, and you always protect me from evil. I still have much to learn, and I will never stop believing. Today, Lord, please help me ...

_____

_____

_____

_____

In Jesus' name I pray. Amen.

Day 179

Look, God is all powerful.

Job 36:22 TLB

Dear God,

You are the almighty! You made me out of love, and you want me for your own. I want you, too! Today, Lord, I praise you …

_____

_____

_____

_____

In Jesus' name I pray. Amen.

Dear God,

I want to share you with everyone I know. I don't always know how, but you keep teaching me. I want everyone to know about your love. I want them to feel safe and loved. Then maybe there will not be so much craziness in this world. Today, Lord, please help me ...

_____

_____

_____

_____

In Jesus' name I pray. Amen.

"So go and make followers of all people in the world."
Matthew 28:19

Reference Guide to Texas Senate Bill 83

Filed with the Secretary of the Senate on November 12, 2002, by Senator Jeff Wentworth from San Antonio.

Passed the Texas State Senate on April 8, 2003

Passed the Texas House of Representatives on May 9, 2003

Signed by Governor Rick Perry on May 28, 2003

Effective September 1, 2003

Pertinent excerpt from the law: "(d) The board of trustees of each [A] school district shall [may] provide for the observance of one minute [a period] of silence at each school in the district following the recitation of the pledges of allegiance to the United States and Texas flags under subsection (b). During the one-minute period, each student may, as the student chooses, [the beginning of the first class of each school day during which a student may] reflect, pray, [or] meditate, or engage in any other silent activity that is not likely to interfere with or distract another student. Each teacher or other school employee in charge of students during that period shall ensure that each of those students remains silent and does not act in a manner that is likely to interfere with or distract another student."